Hot and Cold Poems

Compiled by John Foster

KV-063-065

Contents

Acknowledgements

The Editor and Publisher wish to thank the following who have kindly given permission for the use of copyright material:

John Foster for 'That's hot', 'In the desert', 'Summer and winter', 'The snowman says', 'Keeping warm' and 'On cold winter nights' all © 1994 John Foster; Tony Mitton for 'Don't touch' © 1994 Tony Mitton; Irene Yates for 'Ice lolly' © 1994 Irene Yates.

That's hot

Flames from a dragon.
Water boiling in a pot.

A blazing fire.
The desert sun.
That's hot!

John Foster

3

Don't touch

See that porridge,
bubbling in the pot?
Don't touch the pan.
It's very hot.

Mind that bag
of fish and chips.
Blow on them first,
or they'll burn your lips.

Don't touch that kettle.
It's got hot water in.
Keep away from the fire.
You could burn your skin.

This is something
you all must learn.
Don't touch hot things,
because they burn.

Tony Mitton

In the desert

In the desert,
Some rocks get so hot
In the sun,
That you could fry
An egg on one!

John Foster

8

Ice lolly

Ice lolly,
lick it quick,
before it drops
off the stick!

Irene Yates

Summer and winter

In winter,
It is so cold
That the water in the lake
Freezes into a thick slice
Of ice.

In summer,
It is so hot
That I take my shirt off
And jump in the pool
To get cool.

John Foster

11

The snowman says

I like it when it's cold,
When the north wind blows,
When it snows and it freezes
My nose and my toes.

I don't like it when it's hot,
When it's sunny all day,
When my nose is runny
And I melt away.

John Foster

Keeping warm

I wish I had
Thick white hair,
Like a polar bear,
To keep me warm
When the cold wind blows
And it snows.

But my skin is thin,
So I have a thick coat
To wrap myself in,
To keep me warm
When the cold wind blows
And it snows.

John Foster

On cold winter nights

On cold winter nights
it freezes and snows,
and my hot water bottle
toasts my toes.

John Foster

Printed in Hong Kong